S0-CPE-461

# A BATH FOR RAGS

by Mary Beth Spann

Rags was sad.

He did not want a bath.

Rags ran.

He ran on a mat.

He ran on a hat.

Rags ran and ran.

He ran by a can.

He ran by a fan.

Rags ran and ran and ran.

He ran in the van.

He ran in the sand.

Rags ran and ran and ran and ran.

BAM! Rags ran into Sam.

Splash! Rags had a bath.

Sam had a bath, too!